It's Not You–It's Them

Six Choices to Healing & Thriving After Abuse

Cover Art: Justin James

ISBN: 0615515649

ISBN-13: 978-0615515649

Victoria Roder

Victoria Roder

D W B   P U B L I S H I N G
www.dancingwithbearpublishing.com

Victoria Roder

Life has been an interesting ride, but everything in it, good and bad has brought me to a place where I know my eternal salvation is found in Christ. I'm still a work in progress, but I'm getting there. Praise to the Father that created me and the Son that has redeemed me. In this I can be joyful.

Thank you to everyone that answered my surviving abuse survey. Melissa, Marie, Pam, and Wendy for allowing me to quote you're words and share your struggles. You are helping others to heal through your experiences. May God's grace shine upon you.

I am so grateful for the men in my life that have shown me God's love and grace. My "new dad" Vel; my father-in-law Darrel; and the love of my life, Ron.

May the God of hope fill you with all joy and peace as you trust in Him, so you may overflow with hope by the power of the Holy Spirit.

Romans 15:13

And we know that in all things God works for the good of those who love Him who have been called according to his purpose.

Romans 8:28

Victoria Roder

1. Attitude

2. God's Plan

3. Worthiness

4. Forgiveness

5. Learning to Trust

6. Joyful Living

Victoria Roder

~ Choice One ~

Attitude

You can't change your past, but you can choose your future.

Attitude!

Good or bad our circumstances may influence who we are, but each of us are responsible for who we become. Here's a good piece of advice I've heard that I'd like to share - "be in control of your attitude, or it will control you."

Our parental relationships directly affect our personal relationships with others, and with God. We grow to have either mature relationships with others, and become loving, caring, trusting adults, or we wind up on the opposite end and are unable to accept love from others, or from God.

As a former child of abuse, I asked other victims a few questions about their experiences. The volunteers were eager to share their life stories with the hope that those experiences would help others heal.

In regards to relationships on the survey, Melissa said, "...I have a history of sabotaging relationships."

There it is. Poor parental relationships affect your personal relationships in the future.

You will make a choice, it will take effort but you can choose to heal yourself, and choose to have mature relationships by choosing your attitude.

Yes, face it. Own up to it, regardless of what has happened to you in the past - happy, sad, contentment, dissatisfaction, or anger, we choose our attitudes, which can hinder or enhance our relationships with others.

I'm not a psychiatrist, psychologist, or a therapist, so what advice can I give someone else about surviving abuse and healing their heart?

My answer is life experience.

I was born into an abusive home and then, as fate would have it, I was sent to an abusive foster home that was even worse. Finally, I was rescued by my current family. In the trauma that marked my beginning, God's words from Romans 8:28 are fulfilled.

"And we know that in all things God works for the good of those who love him, who have been called according to His purpose."

Becoming a man or woman of God requires letting go of all the harmful traits we have been taught in our lives, becoming a child again, and relearning childhood traits that were never taught us. We must learn the difference between fearing God and being *afraid* of who God is. We must understand who God is, as well as Christ's nature and character.

Nature verses nurture. A past of physical, emotional, verbal, and sexual abuse can sometimes be the making of a social deviant. So, why am I a productive member of society and the next abused, abandoned person is a serial killer?

My answer is a Bible based faith in God.

Maybe you weren't blessed with family or friends that could share Christ with you, but as an adult, you can choose to read your Bible, find a church, and fellowship with other believers to grow and change in Christ.

I was blessed to be adopted into a family with a solid foundation of Christ as the anchor. Sure, there were times I felt dragged to church. My adoptive parents weren't just Sunday morning Christians - they lived what they believed on a daily basis.

My adoptive dad was the, "You live under my roof, you live by my rules," man. He was strict but consistent and fair. You knew where you stood because actions had consequences and those consequences were always the same. It wasn't the nerve wracking dysfunction of guessing if an infraction was overlooked one day, and severely punished the next day.

I was thrilled to have my personal story of adoption published in the anthology entitled, <u>A Cup of Comfort for Adoptive Families</u>. My story, *Why I Believe in Angels* is the account of how I came to live with my current family at the age of seven. I'm thankful that my adoptive family chose to bring this heartbroken, hard-to-place little girl into their lives for the long haul.

That publication has inspired many people to share their own stories of adoption with me. Heartfelt tales told through the eyes of parents and also from the children that were adopted. I am sorry to report I also heard a few troubled stories of adoption and one comment remained in my thoughts and stalked me.

The reader felt resentful that her biological aunts, uncles, and grandparents never made an effort to adopt her, or keep in touch with her. Her story was in total contrast to my adoptive family. My "new" family made me believe in angels on earth.

That sole comment and my personal experience spurred an idea and became the dispositions for Detective Leslie Bolt and her sister Tasha in my novel, **Bolt Action**, Champagne Books 2010.

In Bolt Action, the sisters were both adopted at the age of seven by James and Ruth Bolt. Leslie is a sarcastic loner but grateful to her adoptive family. Tasha is bitter and resentful at the unfortunate circumstances that dictated her life and attempts to cover her bitterness with shallow relationships.

The main premise of the novel may be a serial murder mystery but the character development of the sisters focuses on how each sister individually deals with her troubled past in relationship to her current life. So, what's the difference between the Bolt sisters?

Attitude.

One sister is grateful and one sister is bitter. So remember, you choose your attitude. Choose either a negative or positive attitude but own up to your choice. You can't change your past but you can choose your future.

~ Choice Two ~

God's Plan

Perhaps you have endured condemnation, harsh words, and neglect. Abuse, whether physical, verbal, sexual, or a combination, directly affects a child's view of themselves and God. We are raised according to the parents we are given, whether they be drug addicts, Christians, or kind, secure, responsible people. These first views of our parents set the pattern for how we see ourselves, and set the course for future relationships, as well as our view of God.

Matthew 18:3 states: And He said, "Truly I tell you, unless you change and become like little children, you will never enter the kingdom of heaven."

The verse says, *unless you change*, and change constitutes making an effort. The Lord was convicting me to deal with my past but as a former withdrawn child, I am an expert at denial and avoidance. Perhaps withdrawal is a coping mechanism God equipped me with to survive. Confrontation on any level, including confrontation with the past, is difficult for me to cope with but I haven't been able to find anywhere in the Bible where it says that life will be easy or confrontation free.

The Bible verse I have chosen as my life verse is Jeremiah 29:11. "For I know the plans I have for you, declares the Lord, plans to prosper you and not to harm you, plans to give you hope and a future."

Nope. The verse doesn't say anything about God's plans being easy. It is God's plan for life but each of us has to do the work. God calls us to be an active participant, not a bystander in life.

Concentrate on these words from the book of Jeremiah... "Plans to prosper you declares the Lord."

Wow! The Lord that created the heavens and the earth has plans for little o' me. I'm one person out of billions and yet, He knows me by name. But remember, Jeremiah 29:11 doesn't say I know the plans I have for Victoria Roder only, so you can claim this verse as your own promise from God.

"...plans to give you a hope and a future."

Wow, again! The God that delivered the Israelites, saved Noah from the flood, and gave man the ability to mass produce chocolate, promises to give me a hope and a future.

Who am I to doubt God? Didn't He promise the rainbow and send it? Didn't He promise to send His only Son to die in my place and then send Him? Christ promised He would rise from the dead and He did. Why can't I, after knowing God keeps his promises, have hope in the future He promised me?

I asked the survey participates to share a Bible verse that brings them comfort when they are down.

Pam shared, "Be still and know that I am God." Psalm 46:10

Melissa shared 1 Peter 5:6-7, Therefore humble yourselves under the mighty hand of God, that He may exalt you in due time, casting all your care upon Him, for He cares for you.

My natural tendency is to lose sight of God's promises because His ways are not my ways. If I designed my life, would I have chosen to start with one family and then wind up with another? No. I would have never seen that as an option. I would have just given my sweet, little, baby-self to my adoptive family.

But how would that have changed God's plan for my life and the people that have been affected by, and intersected with, my life? Think about the chain reaction.

If I had been born into my adoptive family, I would lose three sisters and a brother that I love dearly. I would never have been able to donate my almost perfectly matched kidney to my biological sister. What would have happened to her life?

Think of all the people you meet, and although you don't always know how, you definitely affect their life. Change something about your life and that affects others, and the change reaction goes on and on.

How would changing my origins have altered my personality? Would I have the same compassion for children? Would I be speaking out in my novels and blogs to bring self-acceptance and hope to adult survivors of child abuse? Would I be this chubby? Oops, sorry. That topic creeps into my mind at the strangest times.

"For my thoughts are not your

thoughts, neither are your ways my ways," declares the Lord. Isaiah 55: 8.

Clearly, left to my own, I tend to screw things up in my flawed ability to see the big picture. For example, as children, my siblings and I thought it would be a good idea to tie bed sheets together and climb out of a two story window to the ground. Not too smart. As fun as scaling the outside of your house sounds to kids, we did not consider the whole picture. Although our parents where nowhere to be found, the horrified neighbors where home and able to report back to them!

A few of my choices in friends and boyfriends haven't been the wisest decisions in my life. Don't tell my "new" parents, but maybe they were right about a few of my choices. A poor choice in partners seems to be a pattern for people who have been abused.

From the survey I sent out, Marie said

she was, "...always hooking up with destructive men who also abused me..."

His ways are not our ways. If I keep doing the same thing, I'll get the same results. One of my sisters was stressed about the direction her life was going. Like any sarcastic sibling, I gave her a little advice. I asked her why she didn't ask God to help her handle her life and get it turned around.

She replied, "I'm used to doing things my own way."

In sisterly support, I said, "Oh, and that's working so well for you?"

Are you trying to solve all your problems on your own? Are you keeping your burdens to yourself instead of turning them over to God? How well is that working for you? Common sense dictates if you keep doing the same thing, you will get the same result. So, how do you let go and accept God's plan for you?

Pray, pray, pray, and then pray some more. Sometimes we don't know what to ask for or what we truly need. That's okay, God has that covered, too.

"In the same way, the Spirit helps us in our weakness. We do not know what we ought to pray for, but the Spirit himself intercedes for us with groans that words cannot express. And he who searches our hearts knows the mind of the Spirit, because the Spirit intercedes for the saints in accordance with God's will." Romans 8: 26-27

Maybe you don't know what to pray because you aren't sure what is lacking in your life. Perhaps you are too emotionally exhausted to pray, or you're not sure what it is that's bothering you.

Remember Romans 8 states - the Spirit intercedes on your behalf. Relax, God has thought of everything. God even knew you might be at the end of your rope and not know how to ask for help.

I am reminded of the children's song with the line... "My God is so great, so strong and so mighty there's nothing my God cannot do."

His plans may not be my plans, but I know that His plans are more than I could ever have imagined for my life.

Keep in mind praying doesn't mean the person that abused you will change. Perhaps your perpetrator passed away and you never had the opportunity to confront them.

The majority of the survey participants never had the chance to confront their abuser, but say they would like to be given that opportunity. The few individuals that did confront their abuser were not satisfied by the confrontation, and did not feel validated, or experience closure.

Even if you didn't have the chance for closure, keep praying and eventually you will be able to let the pain go. With the help of God, through the blood of Christ, you can accept that the abuse wasn't your fault. You may feel unlovable but God finds you worthy to love.

Ephesians 1:18-19 says, "I pray also that the eyes of your heart may be enlightened in order that you may know the hope to which He has called you, the riches of His glorious inheritance in the saints, and His incomparably great power for us who believe. That power is like the working of His mighty strength."

Knowing the hope and the power of His mighty strength will help you accept God's plan for your life.

~ Choice Three ~

Worthiness

Psychiatrists say sarcasm is a form of anger. You know, they make it sound like sarcastic humor is a bad thing. I have to bite my tongue a lot. It's not right but sarcastic thoughts come out of no where and posses me. I have to fight to keep them inside remembering that God tells us to guard our words.

I have a friendly hint for you - don't ask me if I like your haircut. Relax—I'm kidding. The truth is, the person I'm most sarcastic toward is myself. Perhaps it stems from the realization that my own father, and then my first foster parents couldn't have cared less if I died. There were even a few times I believed they were trying to speed that process along.

The acceptance of that realization, or

belief that someone thinks so little of you that they can easily abuse or belittle you, can lead to an unhealthy view of self-worth. Lack of self-value can lead to destructive be-haviors. In my survey, I asked the survivors of abuse if they went through any stages of destructive behavior in their lives.

The common answers where, drugs, alcohol, promiscuous behavior, suicide attempts, and eating disorders. The devil knows our weaknesses and he whispers the feelings of self-doubt, lack of self-worth, and abandonment issues, into the depths of our souls.

Wendy replied in her survey that she had a lot of destructive behaviors because, "...I always felt like I needed to fit in."

As a child of God, how do you defeat those negative feelings when Satan is shouting them in your ear?

Psalm 139:14 tells us, I praise you because I am fearfully and wonderfully made.

Our worthiness isn't contingent on anything we have done or by our talents. We should all shout for joy that our worthiness isn't based on how other people treat us. My value and yours, comes from the Father that created us and the Savior that washed us perfect in His blood.

"I praise you because I am fearfully and wonderfully made." Psalm 139:14

My Father in Heaven doesn't see you or me as disposable, or as a burden that perhaps our parents or a partner might.

If you are an adult survivor of child abuse, or dealing with spousal abuse, it is difficult to not ask the questions, "What did I do to cause this? What could I have done differently?"

In the circumstance of abuse, I want

you to know it's not you–it's them. I repeat, *It's Them*! Don't give Satan the power by blaming yourself. Satan wants you to blame yourself, and he wants you trapped in the past so that you don't claim your promises from God and live a joyful life.

Choose to claim God's affirmation that you're fearfully and wonderfully made. You can't control how someone else treats you. You can only control your reaction to them. As an adult, you can choose who you will allow into your life. Sometimes, for our own well-being, we must distance ourselves from certain people.

The following is a dream sequence from my novel, **The Dream House Visions and Nightmares**, Asylett Press July 2009. It is a fictionalized account of the domestic violence my siblings and I survived from our childhood. For this novel I researched dream meanings and according to dream analysts, in a dream a bat symbolizes an evil working against you, snake means treachery, and rats foretell of serious trouble to come.

The man stumbled past me. I could smell a mixture of stale beer and cigarettes in the breeze left behind in his haste.

He doesn't see me.

Again everything was a blur, and I hadn't noticed the children until he seized them, one by one, clutching whatever part of them he could get a hold of–the oldest girl by her hair, the little blond girl by the nape of her neck. He tossed the young boy into the line up by his shirt collar. He pushed each one up against the void wall in the living room. I could hear whimpering, but the children appeared too frightened to release much sound.

He loaded his .357 Smith and Wesson as he said, "I told you to be quiet but I heard singing. Someone needs to tell me who was singing."

A bat flew across the desolate room. It appeared as though the children never saw it swoop past them. Their tear-stained faces never flinched as the nocturnal mammal perched on the enraged man's shoulder.

Motionless, each child stared down at the stained mustard-yellow colored carpet. The cock of the gun echoed in my ears. The sadistic man raised the barrel and—with deliberate slow motion—he aimed the gun at each child. They stood motionless.

A shot rang out, and I felt my heart skip a beat. The children flinched, but no one screamed... except me. To my amazement, no one seemed to hear me. No one was aware of me. More strangely, none of the children ran for cover. The bullet tore into the non-decorated wall, next to another bullet hole already there.

The man's big, meaty paw snatched the little boy out of the line up and shoved him to the dirty floor. The bat stretched its wings but continued to cling to the man's shoulder. The overbearing man never noticed the blood that trickled through his shirt, drawn by the bat's claws. He kicked the young boy in the stomach with the toe of his cowboy boot. Instantly, the boot transformed into a snake. It recoiled, drew back, and struck the cringing child.

Now, without hesitation, the oldest girl stepped forward. "It was me. I was singing."

The beer-bellied man waved his tattooed arm and without making a sound the younger children morphed into rats, and scurried out of the room.

Another shot rang out.

~ * ~

Perhaps you can relate to this mistreatment on some level. Physical, emotional, verbal, and sexual abuse all affects our perception of ourselves and the world around us.

Issues of self-worth, trust, perception of love, attachment, and bonding can become distorted or dysfunctional. What can you do about those feelings and doubts, and how can you heal? In confidence, claim your worthiness through your Savior, Christ Jesus.

I believe what God told Jeremiah still rings true for the followers of Christ today... "Before I formed you in the womb I knew you." Jeremiah 1:5

He knew you before you were even created in the womb. God doesn't want you to be fearful, sad, and self-loathing. He is convicting you to heal through Christ and live the full and joyful life you have been promised and richly deserve. Even if you have to do it every new day, remind yourself, you deserve a joyful life!

First, choose your attitude, seek out God's plan for your life, follow it, and then confirm your worthiness in Christ. And now, for the hard part... forgiveness, learning to trust, and joyful living.

~ Choice Four ~

Forgiveness

It may hurt you when I discuss the dynamics of Bible-based forgiveness. You may not be ready to forgive unspeakable things that you have been forced to endure. By suggesting forgiveness for the perpetrator, I am not dismissing the trauma you have suffered. But in truth, hanging onto the pain of abuse may be a crutch, and the crutch becomes your comfort because that's what you know. Hanging onto the fear, abandonment, and anger is holding you back from a life of true joy.

Bear with each other and forgive whatever grievances you may have against one another. Forgive as the Lord forgave you. Colossians 3:13

God has convicted me to write about abuse and healing just as he is convicting your heart to read and accept His word, love, grace, and power. We are all capable of pretending happiness on the outside. What I am suggesting is that if you turn the pain over to God instead of keeping it for yourself, you will be able to say - the past doesn't matter.

Traumatic experiences should make us stronger, not weaker. Good and bad, all of our experiences are a part of who we are.

This verse from Colossians doesn't say, continue a relationship with a person that is harming you and continue to be abused.

Anytime in your life, if you fall victim to abuse, you need to seek help immediately. Your abuser may never admit what they have done to you, and it is possible they will never request forgiveness. That doesn't mean you can't give it over to God.

You can forgive someone for abusing you, but that doesn't guarantee the abuser has, or ever will, change. That doesn't mean you can't let it go. Forgiveness doesn't imply the person will never attempt to hurt you again. It simply means you forgive them for what they have done to you, and then you choose to move on with your life, your sanity, and your well-being.

"For if you forgive men when they sin against you, your heavenly Father will also forgive you. But if you do not forgive men their sins, your Father will not forgive your sins." Matthew 6:14-15

This verse doesn't say only forgive people of infractions that are easy to forgive. This verse isn't a suggestion. It is cause and effect. If *you* forgive, your Father in heaven will forgive you.

If you feel you are not ready to follow God's direction for forgiveness, I want you to consider Jonah and Saul. They certainly were not ready to follow God when He began convicting their hearts.

If God is tugging at your heart, He is preparing you for the tough part of learning to forgive, trust, and live a joyful life. I assure you that if you pray, and pray some more, and believe this burden will be lifted from your heart, the God that intervened and changed Saul's heart on the road to Damascus from persecuting Christians, to Paul the Great Apostle, can also heal your heart.

But He said, "Blessed rather are those who hear the word of God and keep it!" Luke 11:28

"Do not repay evil with evil or insult with insult, but with blessing, because of this you were called so that you may inherit a blessing." 1 Peter 3:9

There were times in my life where I thought I would have liked to see a foster family I was placed with suffer. I wanted them to be humiliated as they humiliated me, perhaps see them physically harmed as they harmed me, or at least punished for their mistreatment of me, a helpless child.

I couldn't comprehend their treatment. I'm certain the social worker informed them of the trauma I had already suffered at the hands of my own father. At six years old, my mother was dead, I was separated from my sisters and brother, although also children, the only people I knew and trusted. Yet these foster parents that promised the state they would care for me, were incapable of showing me any compassion, and chose to further abuse an already broken child.

It is strange but I didn't wish my own abusive father harm or punishment. Perhaps that was another gift or coping mechanism from God. All I ever wanted from my own father was for him to realize, before he died, that I am worthy of love and I am a valuable human being. To my knowledge, that never happened.

Melissa also said in her survey that if she could ask her abuser anything without repercussions, it would be, "... did you ever really love me?"

In this life time, we may never know the answers we think we want but God's ways are not my ways. I have learned and accepted that it doesn't matter if my biological father loved me. My Father in Heaven loves me, and has a purpose and a plan for my life. What man intended for evil He has turned to good.

I'm not a child anymore, I'm not helpless, and through my faith in God, and the comfort I find in my Savior, the past doesn't matter. I am choosing a future of joyful living, and so can you.

~ Choice Five ~

Learning to Trust

"This is the confidence that we have toward Him, that if we ask anything according to His will He hears us." 1John 5:14

Often women marry seeking a man to become the father she never had, wanting that knight in shining armor. Yet, at the same time, they are insecure, distrusting, and waiting for the man in their life to fail.

Men often marry the woman who will replace the mother in their life. Those who were raised in an abusive family life, where their father hit or beat their mother, often become abusers. They are insecure about being left by their wives, they become controlling, abusive husbands and fathers. These men often have such a skewed concept of self, and what being a "man" means, that they have no concept of God.

As we travel through some of life's experiences, we may question if we will survive. Think of the old saying, *what doesn't kill you, makes you stronger*. You're reading this, so you survived. Ask yourself - do you want to just survive or do you want to thrive?

Holding onto the pain of the past can lead to the self-destructive behaviors of addiction, and the alienation of relationships. We already discussed choices, so make your choice. If you want to thrive you need to forgive, leave the pain behind, and learn to trust.

Learning to trust was not something that came automatically for me. I had to ask God to grant me the ability to not condemn people that have not personally harmed me.

Sometimes, as Christians, we don't stand up for ourselves and certain people will take advantage of our kindness. I'm not suggesting you have to trust your perpetrator or set yourself up for vulnerability. You can be a Christian and still be strong and make wise decisions. I'm suggesting you learn to trust people again, so that you don't heap your past hurt, pain, and abandonment issues into your new relationships.

Everything you've experienced is a part of who you are but recognize when it's your insecurities and past making you fearful. I'm sure each of us who has been abused, have heaped a few issues on our significant others when they were late for dinner.

The devil is there to shout the fear of abandonment and feelings of worthlessness into our ears. But if we can recognize those insecurities for what they are, cut ourselves a little slack as we train ourselves to trust, and ask forgiveness when we heap our fears onto unsuspecting bystanders, we can conquer the past.

"When I am afraid, I put my trust in you." Psalm 56

~ Choice Six ~

Joyful Living

"A happy heart makes the face cheerful, but heartache crushes the spirit." Proverbs 15:18.

Heartache can crush your spirit and make it a struggle to get out of bed in the morning and fulfill routine tasks. You barely drag yourself through the day and then dread the next day before it has even begun. It doesn't have to be that way, make a choice.

Our joy isn't contingent on our life circumstances but our Joy comes from the Lord. Our joy isn't in this world, but in the next.

"May the God of hope fill you with all joy and peace as you trust in him, so you may overflow with hope by the power of the Holy Spirit." Romans 15:13

Overflow with hope. From Webster's New World College Dictionary the definition of hope is... "a feeling that what is wanted is likely to happen; desire accompanied by expectation."

Overflow with hope. Does it get any better than that? If we don't have hope, what do you have? I believe lack of hope is why people succumb to suicide. Surviving isn't enough for me, I want to thrive.

"I came that they may have life and have it more abundantly." John 10:10

"My grace is sufficient for you, for My power is made perfect in weakness." 2 Corinthians 12:9

Grace means undeserved favor. My grace is sufficient for you. Say it again. My grace is sufficient for you. What does that mean to me? Oh dear, that's sounds like my Lutheran upbringing, as I memorized the commandments. Sufficient grace.

Can it really be that simple? Yes, it can. I believe God is telling me I don't have to carry the burden of someone else's actions, and I don't have to worry about the pain from the past, the humiliation, the fear of rejection, or even trouble in the future.

It wasn't me. It was them! How freeing those few words are. I want to shout it in the street and from the mountaintop. It wasn't me, it was them - their problems, their issues, and their sins. Yes, call it what it is, *their sin*. I am not responsible for anyone else's actions, only my own actions and re-actions.

"Cast all your anxiety on him because he cares for you." 1 Peter 5:12.

I am still a work in progress. One day I'm joyful, the next day I falter and let the devil convince me I am worthless. He likes to remind me that my own parents didn't love me.

As a work in progress, day after day, I cast the burdens of abuse, fear, humiliation, and abandonment at the foot of the cross. His grace is sufficient and I choose joy. I can choose joy by accepting the truth according to scripture.

I know that in the heart of God I was fearfully and wonderfully made. I know that although his ways are not my ways, God has a plan to prosper me and give me a hope and a future. I choose forgiveness of those who have sinned against me to set myself free to joyful living.

My God saved Noah and his family from the flood, and he will save me from my own fears and self-doubt. In the comfort of my Savior Christ Jesus, I choose a life of joy in the affirmation that it wasn't me-it was them, their problem, and their sin. It wasn't me—it was them. You can't change your past, but you can choose your future.

~ Bible Study and Discussion ~

It's Not You – It's Them

What are the six steps to healing and thriving after abuse?

1.

2.

3.

4.

5.

6.

Look up, memorize, and write on your heart: Romans 8:28

"And we know ____ __ ___ _____ ___

____ ___ ___ ____ __ _____ ___ ____

___, ___ ____ ___ _____ _____ __

___ _____.

Look up Matthew 18:38. What must we do, and what must we become to enter the Kingdom of Heaven?

Discussion:

In a religious sense, what do you think becoming like a child means?

If we want to know and follow God's plan for our life it is important to pray. Based on Romans 8:26-27, who intercedes for us if we don't know what to pray?

Claim your worthiness in the Father that created you and the Savior that washed you perfect by His blood. Look up and record Psalm 139:14

"I _____ ___ _____ _ __ _____
___ _____ ____."

Based on Matthew 6:14-15 - If you forgive, what promise does God give you?

If you don't forgive, what will you be denied?

Discussion:

Is it harder for you to ask forgiveness or grant forgiveness?

What is the hardest part about forgiving someone?

What is the definition of Hope?

You can't change your past, but you can choose your future. Look up the verses below. Claim your worthiness in the God that created you and the Savior that redeemed you, and live a joyful Life:

Ephesians 1:18-19

John 10:10

Proverbs 3:5-6

~ Bible Study Answer Key ~

It's Not You – It's Them

Six steps to healing and thriving after abuse.

1. Attitude

2. God's Plan

3. Worthiness

4. Forgiveness

5. Learning to Trust

6. Joyful Living

Romans 8:28

"And we know that in all things God works for the good of those who love him, who have been called according to his purpose.

Matthew 18:3

To enter the Kingdom of Heaven we must change and become like children.

Discussion:

Trusting and unpretentious like children

Romans 8:26-27

The Spirit intercedes for us.

Psalm 139:14

"I praise you because I am fearfully and wonderfully made..."

Matthew 6:14-15

If you forgive, God promises to forgive you, and if you don't forgive others you will be denied forgiveness

Discussion:

Open

Definition of Hope:

A feeling that what is wanted is likely to happen; desire accompanied by expectation.

Hope

Intersect the number and the bold letter to find the letter to place on the corresponding lines below to solve the puzzle.

	A	B	C	D	E
1	R	L	E	9	T
2	F	H	G	A	B
3	C	M	Z	K	U
4	N	J	W	Q	S
5	Y	X	D	I	V
6	P	7	O	3	4

For I know __ __ __   __ __ __ __ __   __

      1E 2B 1C   6A 1B 2D 4A 4E   5D

__ __ __ __   __ __ __   __ __ __

2B 2D 5E 1C   2A 6C 1A   5A 6C 3E

__ __ __ __ __ __ __ __ __ __ __ __

5C 1C 3A 1B 2D 1A 1C 4E   1E 2B 1C

__ __ __ __ __ __ __ __ __ __ __

1B 6C 1A 5C   6A 1B 2D 4A 4E   1E 6C

__ __ __ __ __ __ __ __ __ __ __ __ __

6A 1A 6C 4E 6A 1C 1A   5A 6C 3E   2D 4A 5C

__ __ __ __ __ __ __ __ __ __ __ __

4A 6C 1E   1E 6C   2B 2D 1A 3B   5A 6C 3E

__ __ __ __ __ __ __ __ __ __

6A 1B 2D 4A 4E   1E 6C   2C 5D 5E 1C

__ __ __ __ __ __ __ __ __ __

5A 6C 3E   2B 6C 6A 1C   2D 4A 5C   2D

__ __ __ __ __ __

2A 3E 1E 3E 1A 1C

Hope

Answer Key:

For I Know the plans I have for you declares the Lord plans to prosper you and not to harm you plans to give you hope and a future. Jeremiah 29:11

About The Author:

Victoria Roder lives in Central Wisconsin with her husband and house full of pets. She is the author of paranormal romance, *The Dream House Visions and Nightmares*, Asylett Press and murder mystery, *Bolt Action,* Champagne Books. She writes articles and creates puzzles for children's magazines. Victoria has two children's books coming out soon.

Visit Victoria at:

www.victoriaroder.com

www.ingramcontent.com/pod-product-compliance
Lightning Source LLC
Chambersburg PA
CBHW060723030426
42337CB00017B/2982